High Praise for Celestial Goddesses . . .

Lisa Hunt celebrates the goddess in her infinite diversity, offering timeless but timely messages from the archetypal world and splendid visions of feminine strength, power, and beauty.

—Patricia Monaghan, author of *The New Book of Goddesses & Heroines*,
The Goddess Path, *The Goddess Companion*, and *Wild Girls*

Provocatively combining spirit and science, *Celestial Goddesses* beautifully illuminates the heavenly powers possessed by women everywhere.

—Kris Waldherr, author of *Sacred Animals*
and *The Goddess Tarot*

Stellar, lovely, and enchantingly written meditations fill the pages of *Celestial Goddesses* to overflowing. Coupled with sensitive, powerful illustrations and myths of the goddess, this book is a charming addition to any library.

—Patricia Telesco, author of *Victorian Grimoire*
and *A Kitchen Witch's Cookbook*

With its beautiful illustrations and empowering meditations, Lisa Hunt's *Celestial Goddesses* is an excellent introduction to experiencing the goddess in her many names and through her many myths from around the world.

—M. Isidora Forrest, author of *Isis Magic:*
Cultivating a Relationship with the Goddess of 10,0000 Names

Lisa Hunt has done a loving service by providing this beautiful guide to the celestial goddesses. Their powerful meditations evoke energies for hope and healing, and lead us on a celestial journey through our inner universe of divine archetypes.

—Amy Zerner and Monte Farber, authors of *The Oracle of the Goddess*,
Gifts of the Goddess Affirmation Cards, and *The Enchanted Astrologer*

With highly visual meditations accompanied by her own visionary paintings, author and artist Lisa Hunt guides the reader in a journey toward self-discovery and empowerment.

—Karri Ann Allrich, author of *A Witch's Book of Dreams*

Lisa Hunt's color portraits evoke the splendor and mystery of these goddesses, and open a path to the heart.

—Galen Gillotte, author of
Book of Hours: Prayers to the Goddess

To Write to the Author

If you wish to contact the author or would like more information about this book, please write to the author in care of Llewellyn Worldwide and we will forward your request. Both the author and publisher appreciate hearing from you and learning of your enjoyment of this book and how it has helped you. Llewellyn Worldwide cannot guarantee that every letter written to the author can be answered, but all will be forwarded. Please write to:

Lisa Hunt
℅ Llewellyn Worldwide
P.O. Box 64383, Dept. 0-7387-0118-1
St. Paul, MN 55164-0383, U.S.A.

Please enclose a self-addressed stamped envelope for reply, or $1.00 to cover costs.
If outside U.S.A., enclose international postal reply coupon.

Many of Llewellyn's authors have websites with additional information
and resources. For more information, please visit our website at
http://www.llewellyn.com

An Illustrated Meditation Guide

Celestial Goddesses

Lisa Hunt

2001
Llewellyn Publications
St. Paul, Minnesota 55164-0383, U.S.A.

FIRST EDITION
First Printing, 2001

All cover and interior illustrations © 2001 by Lisa Hunt
Art direction by Lynne Menturweck
Book design and editing by Rebecca Zins
Cover design by Lisa Novak

Library of Congress Cataloging-in-Publication Data
Hunt, Lisa, 1967–
Celestial goddesses : an illustrated meditation guide / Lisa Hunt.—1st ed.
p.   cm.
Includes bibliographical references.
ISBN 0-7387-0118-1
1. Goddesses—Meditations.   I. Title.

BL325.F4 H86 2001
291.2'114—dc21
2001038014

Llewellyn Publications
A Division of Llewellyn Worldwide, Ltd.
P.O. Box 64383, Dept. 0-7387-0118-1
St. Paul, MN 55164-0383, U.S.A.
www.llewellyn.com

Printed in Canada

For my mother, Annelies,
who nurtured my "wild horse spirit"
and for all of my soul sisters everywhere

Thank You

I would like to thank the following people for their help and encouragement along my journey:

Jon and Connor, "my boys."

Kris Waldherr, "soul sis," for her invaluable input in this project.

Susan Varnum; Pamela Keane of Keane Image; D. J. Conway; Jim Pinto; Mary Claire Hicks; the staff at the Art Institute of Fort Lauderdale; Devon Childress at Lunarace; Lynette and Robert Carsten; Jeff Zurawin; the folks at Llewellyn, including Lynne Menturweck, who has watched me evolve and grow over the years, and Rebecca Zins, Lisa Novak, and Nancy Mostad; and my models, Artiffany, Hagit Brorian, Andrea Salazar, Anna Starling, Susan Varnum, and Yumiko Zurawin.

Special thanks to my family, friends, and fans for their love and support. I appreciate every one of you.

Contents

About the Author

Lisa Hunt has been a professional illustrator for over a decade, with many of her publications reflecting her interest in the feminine divine and the universal themes that are often connected with goddess mythology. Lisa earned a B.S. degree in Computer Animation, worked as a production designer, and has illustrated numerous books, tarot decks, and other products. In addition to her illustrating and writing career, she is an adjunct instructor at the Art Institute of Fort Lauderdale.

Celestial Goddesses represents the culmination of many years of meticulous research and sketching, and showcases Lisa's intense interest in the goddess. Some of her projects include the tarot kits *The Celtic Dragon Tarot* with D. J. Conway (Llewellyn, 1999) and *Shapeshifter Tarot* with D. J. Conway and Sirona Knight (Llewellyn, 1997); the children's book *One Is a Mouse* (Simon & Schuster, 1995); work as a contributing illustrator to the collectible gaming card series *Doomtown* (AEG, 2000), *7th Sea* (AEG, 2000), and *Warlord* (AEG, 2001); and Llewellyn's *2000* and *2001 Tarot Calendar.* To find out more about Lisa and her work, log on to her website: www.lisahuntart.com.

The paintings for *Celestial Goddesses* were executed using transparent watercolors on 100 percent rag hot press watercolor paper.

Preface

When I was in sixth grade, during a conference a teacher told my father that "Lisa has her head in the clouds." I was lost in the universe as my mind drifted out of the classroom window. Over twenty years later, I still have my head in the clouds—except now I realize that what I am seeing just over the horizon is a vast gateway into a world of self-discovery, a territory of endless creative opportunities.

As I grew to recognize the goddess in her manifold forms and guises, I celebrated my own femininity through the creative processes of writing and painting. I have always sketched and painted the ideas that swirled through my mind, but the goddess ultimately became the sound stage for my artistic voice. She was instrumental in allowing me to bloom as a woman and flourish as an artist.

Over time, I realized that I tended to gravitate to goddesses associated with the heavens. The more I contemplated the heavens, the more I connected with my inner being. It became clear to me that the divine energies circulating in the cosmos reflect the mysteries of the feminine divine in all of us. Thus, I developed a great affinity for deities that echoed the rhythms of the universe while reflecting the flow of my own feminine essence.

My desire to understand and to depict her cosmic dance deepened as I gathered information about planetary bodies that the goddess has been associated with in her various incarnations. During my tenure as a computer animation student, I created a three-dimensional animation showing ancient ruins with sacred markings. The heavenly goddess was affecting every creative bone in my body and revealing her many forms in sometimes subconscious ways in my artwork. The goddess was there helping to guide my paintbrush.

Continued research fueled my desire to learn more about the cosmos. As this project was coalescing into a book during the summer of 1999, I had the opportunity to witness a historic moment that perfectly married my passion for the goddess and my interest in space exploration. Standing on my lawn in

Florida, I watched the Space Shuttle *Columbia*, with the first female commander at the helm, emblazon the sky with a brilliant orange streak. As it reached toward the heavens, joy and triumph swelled within me. I sensed the power of the goddess as a fellow woman was reaching for the stars. The goddess and science were uniting to help us understand the mysterious and awesome powers of the universe. It was a symbolic moment that charged me with creative electricity and had a profound effect on my work in the months that followed.

It is my hope that the images in this book will conduct a creative spark that allows you to release your own internal feminine powers. May *Celestial Goddesses* elevate you to new heights of self-awareness . . . and help you to reach for the stars!

Introduction

From ancient mythmakers to modern scientific explorers, human beings have always striven to understand the nature of the cosmos. The sky—with its vast, infinite presence—has inspired awe in all of humanity. Ancient Mayans would literally converse with planetary bodies as they integrated both religious ritual and mathematical equations to predict cosmic phenomena. Humanity has always posed questions about the origins of the universe: Where do we come from? Is the universe self-contained or infinite? Is there a beginning and an end? These are profound questions that have left both mythmakers and cosmologists struggling to grasp the enormity of the universe. The parallels between creation myths and scientific models are closely aligned, and they reflect the universal mystery that compels all of us to want to know why and how we are here. What is our purpose and what place does spirituality and science have in our lives? In Marcelo Gleiser's book *The Dancing Universe*, the author compares the three models of creation myths to the three quantitative models theorized by the scientific community: creation out of something, creation out of nothing, and order out of chaos.

In an attempt to define the mysteries that underlie our existence, we have employed a wealth of symbols and metaphors, including archetypes, symbols that appear throughout human history. Carl Jung, the twentieth-century psychoanalyst, described archetypes as being contained in that reservoir of shared memories passed down through the millennia, our collective unconscious: "The concept of the archetype, which is an indispensable correlate of the idea of the collective unconscious, indicates the existence of definite forms in the psyche which seem to be present always and everywhere" (Jung 42). These archetypal patterns reside deep in the core of our being and surface in dreams, poetry, artwork, and in other forms of creative expression. Myths are part of the psychic heritage that has become embedded in the deep-seated memories comprising our collective psyches. The collective unconscious is what connects us to the past, present, and future, and helps to bind all human beings in a fabric of shared experience.

As we progress down new scientific roads of discovery, there is renewed consideration given to ancient methods of charting celestial movements. Many books focusing on archeoastronomy (the study of astronomical methods utilized by the ancients) share shelf space with books explaining new discoveries and modern theories. We are beginning to see the relevance of connecting with our past as we continue exploring possibilities for the future. Contemplating the divine aspects of our universe is as important as unlocking new theories about its origins. We need the quantitative measures of scientific models to prove theories about the universe. But we also need the mysticism and the human spirit that motivated mythmakers to explain their surroundings. Both disciplines have striven to understand the cosmos. Both disciplines are driven by awe at the immensity of the universe. And neither has been able to prove the origins of the universe. Yet humanity holds on to faith in the face of the inexplicable. As we unlock more answers about nature, we find that there are so many questions lying just beneath the surface. This pattern of question and answer is seemingly infinite, leading one to believe that there will always be a need for both science and faith to help move us forward.

The Space Shuttle *Columbia* on mission STS-93, commanded by Eileen Collins (the first woman at the helm of a space shuttle), launched the Chandra X-ray observatory. The name "Chandra" is a shortened version of the late Nobel Laureate Subrahmanyan Chandrasekhar's name. Chandrasekhar or "Chandra," one of the foremost astrophysicists of the twentieth century, helped shed light on the nature of black holes. Chandra is also a Hindu moon god (in Sanskrit, the word means "luminous"). It is not so ironic that this name was chosen out of 6,000 entries across the country. As we move further into the deep, uncharted realms of the universe, we yearn to embrace the divine as a means of digesting the enormity of the cosmic void. Science is providing us with beautiful, inspiring, visual references of celestial hosts literally billions of light years away. In order to connect with those images and not be too overwhelmed by the confounding distances, we need to celebrate the very mystery of these celestial wonders. Again, we start asking ourselves fundamental questions about our surroundings, much like the ancients did thousands of years ago. Celestial goddesses are like old, consistent friends. Their various roles on the cosmic stage continue to fascinate and reassure us even in the face of scientific challenges. Technology will not supplant our need to nurture our spirituality, it will only reinforce it.

Reverence for the feminine divine is a manifestation of this shared experience. We know intuitively that her power is part of our past, present, and future. The goddess' transformative powers are a part of our daily experience, from the life-giving process of birth to the diurnal cycle dictated by the heavens. The goddess is an inherent part of the cosmic pulse of conception, death, and renewal. This cycle coincides with the phases of the moon, the rising and setting of the sun, and the female menstrual cycle. By reconnecting with the goddess on a conscious level, we begin to truly participate in the mysteries that inhabit our skies and our own internal cosmos. The more we allow ourselves to indulge in the spiritual essence of her presence, the more heightened our senses will become.

It is important to meditate on the goddess as we continue to observe the heavens. The inscrutable nature of the universe is as miraculous as conception and birth. The ubiquitous goddess has given us a wealth of stories and symbols to help us connect with the essence of our souls. The many images and stories that I have presented in this collection showcase the similarities that all goddesses from disparate cultures share. Many of the elements and symbols contained in the paintings represent the merging of the conscious with the unconscious. In the entry for Luonnotar, the Finnish goddess is shown floating upon the primordial waters of chaos until the breaking of eggs releases consciousness and allows life to flourish. Another example of the bridge between unconsciousness and consciousness is exemplified when the Sumerian goddess Inanna breaks away from the smothering embrace of the earth and emerges into a new, conscious state on the surface. The moon and sun are also considered symbols of unconsciousness and consciousness, respectively. Lunar mysteries stem from the fact that the moon is present during the night or unconscious state and the sun coincides with light and consciousness.

The symbolic polarity present in some of my images is a reflection of the balance necessary for the sustenance of life. This can even be observed at the subatomic level. Atoms are comprised of protons, electrons, and neutrons that work together to maintain a neutral charge. Life could not exist without this delicate balance. So, too, the sun goddess' travels across the heavens are juxtaposed by her sojourns under the Earth and into unconsciousness during the hours of darkness. Without light, there would be no dark; without dark, one would not recognize light. The many symbolic images in this book are an attempt to tap into this subconscious level. The paintings are meant to act as tools of contemplation and will hopefully help the viewer identify the nurturing power of the feminine divine. By identifying the beauty and strength that is the goddess, we can learn to harness positive goddess energy and use it to help ourselves become stronger, more intrinsic players in the universe.

The expansion of mass media, the connective capabilities of the World Wide Web, and the ever-advancing space telescopes are leading to profound changes that will forever alter the human landscape. It is the human spirit and our connection with the divine that provides us with the courage to move forward and climb higher pinnacles of achievement.

As we move closer to universal consciousness, what better vehicle for being prepared for such profound thought processes than by contemplating celestial goddesses and their various roles on the cosmic stage? By reflecting on the goddess, we will be better equipped to ponder the complexities of science. In Edward O. Wilson's book *Consilience*, the author states that "science needs the intuition and metaphorical power of the arts, and the arts need the fresh blood of science" (Wilson 230). By depicting the goddess in her myriad of forms and personalities, I am interpreting the divine mysteries of the universe in a tangible form that we all can relate to, regardless of gender or race.

Considering information from complementary disciplines will enable us to grow intellectually as well as spiritually. Contemplating the mysteries of the universe facilitates creative thinking. In true Zen form, the more we learn, the more we need to learn. The internal spirit, the essence of our being, is what is touched by the goddess. If we let our internal voices guide us into pure, contemplative thought processes, then we can examine the quantitative measures of science with an enhanced feeling of awe and reverence. We become more emotionally connected, more spiritually elevated, and ultimately better, more flexible observers of nature. We need the goddess to be a part of our conscious beings as we move forward into a new millennium of astounding scientific discoveries. And as we acquire more scientific understanding about the cosmos, perhaps we can acquire a deeper connection with the goddess.

How to Use This Book

With all the changes that are going on in the world, from technology to our own personal relationships, the one thing that seems to remain fairly constant is the universe. Of course this is not entirely true, but due to our relatively brief physical life spans we can be lulled into the comfortable illusion of cosmic constancy. Human beings are instinctively drawn to the beauty of the stars. We write songs and poems about the glorious sunrise and the romance of a star-strewn night. We are drawn to the mysterious and unattainable nature of the moon and planets. But when we look to the stars and celestial bodies for inspiration, we may also be intimidated by the sheer enormity of it all. It can be difficult not to feel insignificant and downright overwhelmed when contemplating distances that would take a thousand generations to cross. This is the science of the universe as we know it. But where does spirituality fit into this scheme? Is there any room remaining in our fact-jumbled minds for the divine?

Meditation helps us to weed through the detritus of our day-to-day lives in order to get to the pure, creative, fluid part of our mind. This part of our being can be our sanctuary. It is a place where we can explore, nurture, expand, and refresh. It is our personal getaway where no one else has to go. It is our personal playground, a placid beach, a verdant forest, and anything we choose it to be. By going within to this personal and tranquil place, we can see ourselves from a different perspective and perhaps view our life situations with a more objective eye. It is also a place where we can convene with the goddess and contemplate the cosmos.

By employing meditation techniques, we can nurture a relationship with the goddess that can help us to understand our importance in the grand scheme of things. The goddess can provide you with a link to cosmic energy by helping you to explore your own subconscious. Our psyches are like microcosmic reflections of the vast, magnificent universe in which we reside. The goddesses in this collection mirror the patterns or archetypes that surface again and again in world mythologies. By meditating on stories of the goddess, we can allow her to accompany us on our personal quest to understand the nature of the universe and appreciate the limitless knowledge, energy, and creativity contained within our subconscious.

Why Meditate?

Since it is so easy to become distracted by day-to-day concerns, it is important to set aside quiet time to ponder the marvelous goings-on within your own mind. After all, how can we digest the immensity of the universe if we do not take time to nurture our own being? Meditation can help to bring equilibrium and a sense of peace into your life. Through meditation, you will be able to nurture a relationship with yourself by cultivating a relationship with the goddess. The celestial goddess can be a reflection of who we are or who we would like to become.

How to Meditate

No matter how hard we try to balance the complexities of our lives, there is usually something that infiltrates our positive well-being. Perhaps you get stuck in traffic, or you have a falling-out with your best friend, or you burn the beans cooking dinner. No matter how well-managed your life is or how even-tempered you are, it is hard not to experience some level of stress throughout the course of the day. Knowing that you have the option to meditate can help you to deal with your daily mishaps. Meditation is your quiet time. You can look forward to this relaxation time . . . time to recenter and cleanse yourself of your own internal pollution.

When I use the term "meditation," I am not referring to the practices of any particular culture or religion. Meditation is a versatile form of relaxation: You are free to delve into this exercise in any manner that you choose, taking bits and pieces of ideas and practices that feel right to you. You can meditate in the shower, while you walk, or during your lunch break. You can also customize your meditations to include objects, other people, or both.

It may be difficult to get started, but once you incorporate meditation into your routine, it will become a daily ritual that you look forward to. Meditation is also inexpensive—it does not require the inclusion of any instruments or tools.

Meditation can help release creativity and facilitate artistic endeavors, even if you do not have a propensity to express yourself in this manner. I engage myself in a meditative state when I sketch ideas. I feel that the celestial goddess guided my pencil and brush as I painted the images you see in this book. Her image can manifest itself in many styles and forms during this automatic process. But you do not have to be an artist to experience this. You can use meditation as a tool for releasing thoughts and ideas and for helping you to look at your life with a fresh perspective. Daily routines such as cooking, gardening, and shopping can all be enhanced by employing meditation techniques. In Barbara Ardinger's book *Goddess Meditations*, the author states that "meditation is a process whose aim is to quiet the body so the mind can work creatively. It tames the left brain so the right brain becomes free" (Ardinger 10). I find this observation to be quite accurate and useful. I feel it is essential to cleanse my mind by meditating before embarking on a creative endeavor.

Here is a list of techniques that may be helpful for you as you try to determine what techniques best work for your particular needs:

- breathing
- visualization and imagery; this technique is ideal when applied to this book
- taking a walk
- engaging in a creative activity, i.e., sketching, stitching, painting, ceramics, etc.
- positioning yourself: standing, sitting, or lying down
- guided group meditation
- focusing on an object, i.e., a statue of a goddess

Letting the Goddess Work for You

To begin, familiarize yourself with her stories and then study the images in the book. You do not have to be rehearsed in goddess lore or be exceptionally creative, for this book is designed to assist the beginner as well as those who have already established a relationship with the feminine divine. The meditations are meant to be used as a springboard to help you access the wealth of ideas and imagery that are stored within your subconscious, so feel free to expand on what I have provided for you. The more you practice visualization, the more complex and immersive your meditative journeys will become. Visualization, or using imagery to help you with your meditations, is a good technique for those who have a hard time letting go of "reality." The introduction of a visual element will oftentimes help facilitate the relaxation process. It will provide a point of focus— a gateway into the quietude of the subconscious.

It is imperative that you relax and symbolically shed the stresses of the day as preparation for your meditation. I love to take evening walks when the skies are clear and the goddess and the stars speak to me from the blue firmament. Even if I was feeling fatigued or uninspired before my walk, I will often return feeling revitalized and ready to continue writing or sketching. Another of my relaxation techniques is to take a shower in the dark with the window blinds open. This way I can view the stars and moon while the water is cleansing my body (of course, only do this if you feel safe doing so). Try this during the day and you can imagine the sun goddess Saule's golden liquid cleansing you with its nurturing properties. Another way to help prepare yourself for meditation is to take an aromatherapeutic bath with or without strategically placed candles around the tub. I also decorate my home in a celestial motif by hanging moons and stars from the walls and ceilings. These little acts help me to feel peace and harmony within my household. By indulging in these simple pleasures, you can learn how to reestablish inner equilibrium and more easily fall into a meditative state.

My husband uses meditation as a means of organizing his thoughts. He takes daily meditation breaks by lying down on the bed, closing his eyes, and reviewing what he needs to accomplish to clear his "things to do" list. After this refresher, when all his internal papers have been filed away, he will emerge from his meditation reenergized and ready to expedite work in an efficient and relaxed manner. Meditation is an exercise as important as any physical exercise. It is important to keep your mind fit and free of unnecessary stress buildup. If you allow stresses to hibernate in your subconscious without properly disposing yourself of them, you run the risk of depleting your body of good, healthy energy.

You can also incorporate elements from the goddess' stories into your meditation. If you feel you will meditate more successfully by holding or focusing on an object that symbolizes the goddess and her story, by all means do so. For example, White Shell Woman uses a crystal to bring fire to humanity. Try burning a candle and holding a crystal during your journey.

Meditations and visualizations can be performed in group situations or in a solitary manner. I have experienced both and prefer the peace and quietude afforded within my own home. A group meditation can be a wonderful way to feel the transference of energy from one person to another. In the meditation I have provided for Mawu, you can mimic the group circle by meditating with others.

⁓

The goddess' ability to maintain beauty, grace, and strength in the face of adversity reminds us to see the light even during some of our darkest moments. The celestial goddesses are universal yet intensely personal guides who can usher us through our life journeys, helping us to put our fears aside and teaching us how to thrive on challenge. Allow them to aid you in confronting problems in a more effective and rational manner. Above all else, the goddesses remind us that we are not alone in this vast universe. We are the intertwined roots of a grand cosmic tree.

So let us begin. Browse through the book and start with a goddess you feel particularly drawn to. This book is meant to be used over and over again. The more you study it, the more you will be able to extract from the imagery. May you nurture a beautiful relationship with each and every manifestation of the celestial goddess. She has so much to show you.

The Goddesses

Myths
&
Meditations

Amaterasu

Amaterasu, whose name means "Shining Heaven," rules the heavens and brings warmth and light to the world. She is the Japanese Shinto goddess responsible for cultivating rice fields, creating irrigation canals, and teaching mortals the arts of weaving, farming silk, and cultivating food. The great sun goddess was so radiant at her birth that her parents placed her in the sky where she could shine in the celestial realms.

But, alas, her life-giving rays disappeared for a time after her jealous brother Susanowo fell into a rampage and began to destroy Amaterasu's creations. He trampled on her rice fields, left excrement in her temples, and tossed a flayed piebald horse through a roof, killing several weaving women. Amaterasu retreated from the violence by finding refuge in a cave. There she hid herself in protest, causing the world to fall into a wintry plight. Plants began to wither and people began to deteriorate as darkness gripped the land in cold talons.

The gods became alarmed at the dire situation and began to devise a scheme to lure the sun goddess from her cave. The 800 gods gathered around the cave entrance, hung trees with jewels, and placed cocks near the threshold. The erotic goddess Uzume adorned herself with bamboo leaves and began to dance in a manner that created uproarious laughter and cheer. During Uzume's performance, one of the gods placed a mirror in front of the cave entrance.

Amaterasu became curious at the growing ruckus outside her hiding place. She carefully opened the cave door, and there she gazed upon the most beautiful reflection she had ever seen. Amaterasu had never seen herself before, so she was spellbound by her own shining countenance in the mirror. She left the cavernous womb and allowed her brilliant rays to spill upon the landscape. She rejoined the company of the gods and reclaimed her place in the sky. The gods banished Susanowo from the heavens, and life and fertility were restored to the land.

Amaterasu's worship is still honored today, and the Japanese imperial family traces their heritage to the sun goddess.

Guided Meditation

Imagine standing within a damp, chilly tunnel. Darkness feeds your fears as you try to discern a means of escape. Focus hard on a crack in the rock ahead and see a flicker of light. A stream of light expands and permeates the dark cavern. Feel the light beam warm your fingertips and travel up your arms as you begin to move forward. As you lengthen your strides, feel the light continue to travel through your body until it fills your being completely and dissolves the fortress of claustrophobic darkness.

You see an image in the light, and as you squint you can make out your own countenance. It is a smiling reflection of yourself. You look confident, bold, empowered, and beautiful. Walk into your reflection and feel yourself absorbed by the positive solar energy. You feel alive, energetic, brazen. With this new outlook, continue to walk forward into a beautiful, fertile landscape that unfolds before your eyes. You have left the tunnel behind and are now breathing in the fresh, balmy air. Stretch out your arms and breathe deeply; as you breathe out, lower your arms and feel yourself emerge, feeling more confident and alive. Allow yourself to return to your conscious body.

By recognizing the power of your own inner
beauty, you will exude an external beauty
and energy that will enable you to live
more happily and confidently.

Amaterasu

Arianrhod

Arianrhod is the Welsh goddess known as Silver Wheel, who is associated with the moon, night, fertility, magic, and reincarnation. She also is known by the name Silver Goddess of the Dawn.

As the daughter of the great Welsh mother goddess Don, Arianrhod is a beautiful and powerful young deity who lures many seamen into her seductive embrace. Despite her many liaisons with the sea folk, she remains independent and continues to reside in a castle on the secluded island of Caer Arianrhod.

In the *Mabinogion*, a collection of medieval Welsh stories, a story is told of how Arianrhod was summoned by Math, son of Mathonwy, and her brother Gwydion to prove her virginity so that she could provide Math with a lap for his tired feet. She was ordered to step over a rod, but in doing so, she gave birth to two children. One was a blonde boy who crawled away and joined the sea folk to become Dylan-Son-of-the-Wave. The other was a fetus whom Gwydion recognized as his own offspring. Gwydion quickly absconded with the fetus and hid him in a magical chest until the fetus was strong enough to breathe on his own. Feeling violated, Arianrhod exercised a Welsh mother's right to refuse the fetus three things: a name, the right to bear arms, and a human wife. But Gwydion and his son were later able to outwit Arianrhod when they donned disguises and paid her a visit. She inadvertently named the boy Llew Llaw Gyffes, or "The Bright One of the Skillful Hand," after she witnessed the boy kill a wren with a single stone fling. She also provided him with a sword, thus giving him arms. Later Math and Gwydion went to the forest and produced a wife made out of flowers for Llew Llaw Gyffes. The new companion was named Blodeuwedd, or "Flower Face."

It is said that this story illustrates the decline of goddess-oriented societies at the hands of the patriarchal clans. Even so, Arianrhod's status as a deity earned her a place in the constellations as a resident of the Corona Borealis.

Guided Meditation

You are standing on a moonlit mound surrounded by mono-liths engraved with spirals. The goddess Arianrhod appears out of the fog and smiles. She reaches out and you willingly allow her to take your hand. You admire her shimmering presence and feel her tingling energy travel up your arm and into your heart. She leads you to a long branch that hangs down from an ancient tree covered with vines. Arianrhod beckons you to leap over it with her. You try to look past the branch, but are unable to see through a thick fog. You feel a little apprehensive as she leads you forward. You take a deep breath as you jump over. You feel, rather than see, a carpet of stars sweep past your feet. Arianrhod continues to hold your hand as she leads you on a flight past celestial bodies of magnificent col-ors. You see silver wheels spinning past, and time becomes irrele-vant. The new sensation washes away your inhibitions and you feel energized. The wheels continue to float past, and you realize that there are no endings: The wheels turn infinitely, like the continuous birth of stars in an endless universe. Feel your body begin to descend and soon you are back on solid soil. Breathe out and return to your conscious body.

The leap over the branch has shown you that
life is continuous and new beginnings are part
of our journey. Embrace new beginnings and
enjoy the challenges that new flights
will reward you with.

Arianrhod

Artemis

Known as the Greek goddess of the hunt, Artemis protects the animals of the forest and is associated with the bear and the stag. The powerful presence of this lunar goddess sustains wild elemental powers and influences tidal activities, female fertility, psychic abilities, and plant growth. The silver bow and arrows she carries are a gift from her father, Zeus. She was known as Diana to the Romans.

Artemis is both compassionate and vengeful. She is concerned with the sufferings of women and often intervenes during childbirth to help alleviate pain. Immediately after she was born to Leto, Artemis assisted her mother in delivering her twin brother, Apollo. Artemis is a strong, free spirit and she demands respect and chastity from her attending nymphs. She is quick to punish those who challenge her and once shapeshifted her companion Kallisto into a bear for engaging in lascivious behavior with Zeus. Zeus helped Kallisto escape Artemis' wrath by turning Kallisto into the constellation Ursa Major.

Once, while Artemis was bathing by the light of the moon, a young hunter by the name of Actaeon stumbled upon her sacred pool. The young man was paralyzed by the beautiful tableau before him. Realizing that she was not alone, Artemis quickly covered herself and shot at the interloper. The arrow shapeshifted Actaeon into a stag, whereupon his own dogs killed and devoured him.

Even though Artemis rejected marriage and claimed virginity, she fell in love with the god Orion. Her affections for Orion enraged her jealous brother, Apollo. Apollo schemed the demise of Orion by cajoling Artemis to shoot at a distant target in the ocean. Thriving on challenge, Artemis aimed and hit the target—which turned out to be Orion! Realizing her dreadful mistake, she mournfully shapeshifted her dying lover into a constellation and placed him into the sky in the company of his dog Sirius, the Pole Star, and the Pleiades.

Artemis' popularity in the Greek pantheon earned her a prestigious place in the temple of Ephesus. This temple was recognized as one of the Seven Wonders of the Classical World.

Guided Meditation

Behold Artemis as she appears before you. She is strong, muscular, and stands firmly on the moss-covered ground. She begins to walk and you follow her purposeful strides toward a landscape of majestic trees. Your curiosity leads you through a panoply of dazzling light as you explore the wilderness in the company of the goddess. You walk deeper into the forest and the smell of fresh pine captivates your senses. You observe deer nuzzling each other, you see squirrels leap from tree to tree, and your maternal instincts are awakened while watching a bear with its cub. Feel yourself connect with your wild side as you befriend the animals, each representing aspects of your own psyche. The gentleness of the deer, the energy of the squirrel, and the protective nature of the bear encircle your being. The sun begins to set and you no longer see Artemis, but you can feel her presence in the rising moon. You run, gleefully barefoot, toward a running brook. Dip your toes in the water and feel your body become part of the surroundings: You are the running water; you are the crisp, clean air; you are the shafts of moonlight filtering through the leaves. Run your fingers through the soft, moist soil and feel your body becoming part of the earth. Lean back on your dirt-covered hands, let the moonlight revitalize your senses, and breathe deeply. As you exhale, allow your grounded form to return to consciousness.

Communing with nature and allowing
the goddess to help you explore your
wild side will facilitate personal strength,
independence, and fortitude. By indulging
in the untamed feminine, you will be better
equipped to deal with life's challenges
and the many unpredictable roads
that lie ahead.

Artemis

Chang-O

The Chinese revere a deity whose residence on the moon offers comfort and security to the mortals that gaze at her brilliance from below.

Chang-O, or Heng-E as she is sometimes called, once lived with her husband, the famous archer Yi. Yi gained fame and honor when he shot down several suns that were posing a threat to Earth. As a reward, the gods gave him an elixir of immortality that he promptly hid away from his wife, for he did not want to share the potion with her.

During one of his expeditions that kept Yi away from home, Chang-O found the elixir while cleaning. The delicious aroma of the liquid lured the curious Chang-O into taking a sip. She immediately began to feel light and giddy, so she continued to consume the fluid of eternal life. Yi returned from his adventure to find his wife floating effortlessly toward the ceiling. Seeing the empty elixir bottle on the floor, Yi became outraged and tried to catch his wife. When he could not succeed in apprehending her, he took out his bow and arrows with the intention of shooting her down. Chang-O fled out the window and flew upward into the sky toward the light of the moon. Her now-immortal shell made her impervious to the arrows and she landed on the moon unscathed.

Amidst the cold, desolate lunar landscape stood a beautiful cassia tree. The majestic evergreen with its red leaves symbolized renewal and eternal life and was a welcome sight to Chang-O. The branches draped protectively over Chang-O as a hare hopped over to her and introduced himself. He then invited her to live with him in the safety of his lunar palace. There Chang-O helped the hare to manufacture the elixir of eternal life for all women. This elixir brings forth menstruation and ensures fertility, enabling the cycle of life to continue.

People can still see the hare on the dark patches of the moon and are reminded of the life-giving potion that Chang-O helped the hare to create. Moon festivals are held in honor of Chang-O, where women and children participate in parades, eat mooncakes, and celebrate their beloved lunar goddess.

Guided Meditation

Imagine your body drifting upon moonlit ocean waves. You feel the pull of the moon drawing your body out of the water and upward toward the many stars that decorate the universe. You approach the moon and see on its scarred surface a glorious, shimmering castle. You land in the courtyard, feeling light as a feather. You are comfortable in the presence of the structure's warming energy. Breathe in the delicious aroma of cinnamon drifting from the cassia trees lining the courtyard. Chang-O walks from a nearby fountain and holds out a delicate bottle. She offers you a drink after your long journey and you thirstily accept her hospitality. You drink the liquid, feeling warmth spreading throughout your body. Soon energy and light fill your veins with goddess energy. Imagine the bad energy being absorbed by the good energy. You feel cleansed and renewed and are ready to travel back to Earth. You hug Chang-O and begin to rise from the courtyard. Soon you float back down to a beach, where you gently land upon soft, warm sand. Breathe in deeply and allow your body to return to your conscious being.

Nurturing a relationship with the goddess
can help you to replace bad energy with
good, productive energy. It is important
to periodically cleanse yourself of
the negative energy that subtly
accumulates in your subconscious.

Chang-O

Coyolxauhqui

The Aztec moon goddess Coyolxauhqui, whose name means "Golden Bells," shines down upon the people of Earth with her facial bells glimmering in the light. She is an Earth and war goddess who resided on Mount Coatepec with her 400 siblings. Coyolxauhqui was also the only daughter to the famous goddess Coatlicue, or "Serpent Skirt."

A story tells of how the Earth-dwelling Coyolxauhqui assumed the permanent position of lunar deity. Coatlicue, mother of Coyolxauhqui, became pregnant after tucking feathers in her belt. The illegitimate fetus so outraged Coyolxauqui's siblings that they proceeded to plot their mother's demise. Coyolxauhqui fled the circle of conspirators in an attempt to warn her mother, Coatlicue, of her impending doom. When Coyolxauhqui arrived at the mouth of her mother's cave, her half-brother Huitzilopochtli, the sun god, sprang from Coatlicue's womb outfitted in full warrior regalia. He unwittingly attacked his good sister and chopped her into pieces. He then butchered the other siblings in an attempt to prevent future assaults on his dear mother. Coatlicue grieved the loss of her loving daughter. In an attempt to assuage his mother's pain, the remorseful Huitzilopochtli gently placed Coyolxauhqui's head on the moon. Her shining countenance offered her mother comfort during the dark hours of the night.

This story probably uses the vehicle of sibling rivalry to illustrate the constant exchange between night and day. Huitzilopochtli represents the bursting sunshine as he springs from the womb. The 400 siblings, known as "The 400 Centzon Huitznaua," represent stars, and Coyolxauhqui represents the moon. The cyclical nature of the sun slicing through elements associated with darkness parallels the daily cycle of night and day.

Coyolxauhqui's importance in the Aztec pantheon was sealed when archeologists in the 1970s unearthed a large disk portraying the segmented goddess. The fact that the stone disk revealed very little decay could be seen as symbolic of the resilient nature of the faithful moon and the feminine divine that continues to shine upon us.

Guided Meditation

Imagine you are climbing a mountain. The dry air gets cooler and the trees get spindly as you near the summit. Each step becomes more and more tiring and eventually you start to crawl through gravel and dirt. You are about to give in to your exhaustion when a glowing light catches your attention. You stand up straight and try to identify its origins. You feel compelled to climb further. As you reach for the top of the mountain, you are swept away by the vista before you. Clouds begin parting, allowing a brilliant moon to illuminate the valleys. Bells begin to chime and you realize that the moon is in fact Coyolxauhqui. The goddess dominates the night sky and you feel all fatigue from the arduous climb seep out of the soles of your feet. You feel resilient and indomitable as you bask in the goddess' powerful light. You have conquered the mountain and now there is nothing you cannot accomplish. With the help of the goddess' light, the journey will be easier and you are now ready to explore the valleys before you. Sit upon the summit and contemplate the adventures awaiting you. Consider your goals and reassure yourself that they are attainable. Slowly allow yourself to return to consciousness.

Life is full of mountains and valleys.
The goddess can provide you with the
necessary guiding light and energy
to help you reach your goals.

Coyolxauhqui

Hina

Hina is one of the most beloved deities of the Polynesian people. She is a manifold goddess who appears in many myths throughout the Pacific. Her association with the cosmos makes her a preeminent goddess in the Polynesian pantheon. Hina's role as bringer of life, death, and renewal naturally connects her with the waxing and waning of the moon. She also presides over fertility and birth.

It is said that she ventures underneath the lava-rich soil to retrieve water for the Hawaiian people. During her three-day disappearance, darkness descends on the world due to the absence of the moon. Upon her return to the surface, the light of the moon re-illuminates the Earth.

Hina was assigned many roles by the islanders but her most famous persona was that of moon goddess, or "Hina in the Moon." It was said that Hina, growing weary of life as a clothmaker on Earth, decided to sojourn to the sun in her canoe. As she sailed closer to the hot rays of the golden sphere, she decided to change course and traveled to the cooler moon instead. Upon her arrival at the moon, she resumed her profession as a clothmaker.

Other stories expose a more violent transplantation to the cold orb. One day, Hina was industriously beating tapa cloth, much to the chagrin of her brother, Tangora. Her brother became so agitated by the incessant pounding that he lost his temper and ordered his servant to hit the perpetrator of this annoyance. The strike sent Hina sailing across the star-laden sky. Her spirit arrived at the moon, where she continued beating tapa cloth. Perhaps the various incarnations of Hina were meant to mirror the sometimes unpredictable conditions of island life.

Hina can still be seen in the shadows of the moon. Her presence ensures the continuation of life from birth to death to rebirth. Even today, Hina is revered by the Polynesians as a creator goddess of tremendous importance to cosmic balance as well as to everyday life.

Guided Meditation

You are standing in the midst of moonlit tropical splendor. Warm, moist breezes caress your skin and the scent of exotic orchids tantalizes your senses. Before you, ocean waves roar to the shore, stirring your passion for adventure. A canoe approaches and Hina gestures for you to climb aboard. She navigates the seacraft out into the wild waters and soon the shoreline is obscured by ocean spray. The stars reflect upon the surface of the gently rolling ultramarine waves, making it appear as if you were floating in the universe itself. The soft rocking relaxes every muscle in your body as you breathe in the delightful sea air. Hina reaches over the side of the canoe and lifts a long, beautiful cloth that seems to be part of the ocean. She holds out the intricately embroidered cloth and invites you to brush your fingers along the rough tapa. Look at the details and see bits and pieces of your life woven into the fabric. You see your circle of friends, beautiful places you have visited, and everything in your life that has made you feel good. As you continue to reflect on these pleasant thoughts, you notice an area of the cloth that is blank. Examine this patch closely and try to imagine what scenes may be woven in the future. How would you like to improve your life, and what goals would you like to realize to help create a beautiful extension of your life's tapestry? You accept the cloth from Hina and embrace it close to your body. As you breathe deeply, slowly allow yourself to return to consciousness.

Think of your own life as a rich tapestry
waiting to be woven. Think about
what you want your cloth to contain
and focus on the rich interweavings
that are special in your own life.

Hina

Inanna

The Sumerian queen of heaven, Inanna is one of the oldest and most important deities of ancient Mesopotamia. She is associated with love, fertility, birth, death, and rebirth. She wears a crown of stars with a crescent moon and is connected with the cycles of the moon and Venus. She is an earlier version of the Babylonian goddess Ishtar before patriarchal clans influenced her image.

The most famous story about Inanna reveals the universal theme of birth, death, and rebirth that many subsequent pantheons incorporated into their own mythological narratives. Many stories of descent and renewal that followed Inanna's experience bear testimony to the value of universal themes that appear in disparate cultures, the Greek goddess Persephone's journey being the most famous.

Inanna ventured into the bowels of the Earth to visit her sister Ereshkigal, the queen of the underworld. Inanna was forced to relinquish accoutrements of her royalty as payment for her continued passage along the route. She gave up seven items in all before she arrived at her destination. Her sister greeted her with death and immediately hung Inanna's corpse on a meat hook.

Before Inanna's exodus to the dark world, she had instructed her loyal friend Ninshuber to search for her whereabouts if she did not return within a three-day period. As darkness began to descend upon the surface of the world, and plants began to wilt at the absence of nourishing light, Ninshuber knew a terrible fate had befallen Inanna. Ninshuber begged Enki, the god of wisdom, to retrieve the lost goddess from the dark chasms of her sister's domain. Enki agreed and together they traveled to Ereshkigal's chamber and beseeched her to release Inanna. A bargain was struck; Inanna was revived and allowed to return to the surface. As she burst through the outer layers of the Earth's crust, the light of the moon emerged from darkness, initiating fertility and renewal across the land.

Inanna's rebirth is a reminder of the revitalizing power of the female fertility cycle and the important role it plays in all facets of life.

Guided Meditation

Follow Inanna through fossil-lined passageways inside the Earth. You are wearing layers of clothing to help keep yourself warm in the damp, musty environment of rock and soil. As you pass through a doorway, try to let go of things in your mind that are weighing you down and take a deep breath. Breathe out and let these heavy thoughts exit your body. You are feeling warmer and decide to take off a layer of clothing. Leave it behind as you pass into the next chamber. You feel the passageways opening up and soon the air is more plentiful and pleasantly scented. Stop at each doorway and continue to purge your mind of those things in your life that are making the air thick and your feet heavy. Shed the heavy layers that have encumbered your travels along the underground journey. Soon you come upon vast, open landscapes of tree roots. Take in a big gulp of this flower-scented spring air. You only have on a sheath of silk and you feel light of spirit and body. Inanna takes your hand and together you run through the last doorway and burst through the Earth. Warm sunshine spills upon your body. You welcome this new place full of the sounds of spring birds, running water, and gently whispering leaves. You have left the dark womb of the Earth and are embracing the cosmic light of the universe. Behold the pasture of abundant mixed flowers that is spread before you. They contain the colors of your new life palette. As you breathe out, slowly allow your body to return to consciousness.

By imagining your own emergence from the
darkness, you can help alleviate the burden of
your inner detritus that weighs you down and
keeps you in your underground chasms.
Discard unwanted baggage and embrace
the opportunity to start anew.

Inanna

Isis

Isis is one of the greatest and most widely worshipped goddesses of all time. Her influence spread beyond the lands of the Middle East and affected world pantheons well into the Christian era. So powerful is this goddess that she eventually assimilated the attributes of lesser-known gods and became connected with a myriad of names and titles. Her hieroglyphic includes the symbol for throne, evidence of her sublime royal presence.

Isis, the daughter of Nut and Seb, was born on the lucky fourth intercalary day of the Egyptian calendar. She was a loyal and nurturing wife to her brother Osiris, who was king. She presided over governmental affairs during his absence, and assisted Osiris in helping the Egyptian people to become a strong, civilized nation by teaching them the skills of food cultivation, spinning, weaving, astronomy, and medicinal arts. The popularity of the royal couple grew as widespread prosperity extended across the land.

But soon harmony and bliss gave way to great sadness when Set, Osiris' brother, killed Osiris and threw a coffin containing the king's corpse into the Nile. Upon hearing the devastating news, Isis cut off a lock of her hair, tore her own clothing, and embarked on a search for her brother's remains. Upon locating the coffin in Byblos, Isis threw open the lid and engaged in a magical ritual that enabled her to conceive Osiris' heir and future avenger of Osiris' death. But, while hunting under the light of a full moon, Set stumbled upon the cadaver and chopped it up into fourteen pieces. Isis gathered the body parts and performed the first embalming, which was believed to help the deceased travel to the underworld.

Isis' magical skills give her the power to create and restore lives. She is associated with the heavens, the stars, Earth, water, and the underworld, and festivals were held during autumn and spring to honor the omnipresent queen. She was a nurturing mother who was depicted suckling her son Horus. So prominent was this image in the minds of collective psyches that it was incorporated into Christian iconography in the form of the Virgin Mother and Child.

Guided Meditation

You are floating down a river where papyri and flowers line the banks. Isis is navigating the swaying vessel as you watch the gentle ripples reflecting sparkles of sunlight. The goddess guides the boat to the shore and you climb out. Your feet squish in the cooling mud. Squat to cup the clay in your hands. Imagine molding things that are missing in your life or perhaps things that you once had and long to have again. You skillfully build your mud sculpture and pat it as if you are reinforcing these reclaimed pieces of your life, much like Isis reclaimed Osiris. Smell the freshness of the earth and feel that you and your sculpture are connected to everything that is around you. The heat of the sun helps your muscles to relax. Watch the intense rays bake your sculpture. If need be, you can always wet it down again and add to it or change its appearance. When you have finished, cleanse your hands in the water nearby. Feel the soothing liquid wash your hands clean. You feel whole and rejuvenated again as you slowly return to consciousness.

You have the power to mold your life
and reclaim lost dreams. Do not let setbacks
impair your ability to look ahead and envision
a beautiful future for yourself. Your life
sculpture is never completely finished,
but is an ever-evolving work of art
that represents the many dreams,
hopes, and emotions that
comprise your being.

Isis

Luonnotar

The Finnish creator/mother goddess of the heavens known as "Daughter of Nature" floated upon a lonely cosmic sea for 700 years. The winds stroked her and fertilized the waters. She became pregnant with the East Wind's child, but was unable to give birth in the wild primordial waters. Luonnotar continued to drift listlessly, and the baby remained in gestation, as wave upon wave carried her around the infinite ocean.

One day a bird happened upon Luonnotar and decided that her warm lap would provide the perfect nest in the midst of the watery void. Luonnotar was thrilled with the seven beautiful eggs, but in her excitement she inadvertently twitched and broke them. With her life-giving powers, Luonnotar was able to create the sun from the yolks, the moon and stars with the whites, and the Earth from the shells. Luonnotar became creative with her newfound skill and transformed the land into a vista of mountains, rivers, and various geographical wonders. On one of the newly metamorphosed land masses, Luonnotar gave birth to what was to become a great Finnish hero, Vainamonem.

Luonnotar is associated with the heavens, creation, life, the sky, the water, and the moon. She is an important deity in the Finnish-Ugric pantheon in that she helped to create elements of the universe and set all life in motion with her procreative skills.

Guided Meditation

You are floating in the middle of an endless ocean. Your ears are submerged in the chilly water, making everything silent except for the sound of your own heartbeat. You are gazing upon the stars above you as you feel the connection between water and sky. You have been holding an egg in the palm of your hand. The power of the egg lies within its shell. As you close your palm tighter, feel the energy coming out of the egg. The golden contents burst forth and surround your floating form with an intense energy that warms your body. You feel good energy enveloping your consciousness: The stardust of creativity and the wisdom of countless generations contained in the collective unconscious is nourishing your conscious being. Allow these good, healing thoughts to empower you as you slowly return to your waking mind.

You can expand your horizons
by cracking open your inner potential.
Instead of floating along in pools
of stagnation, let your talents bleed beyond
the parameters of expectations.

Luonnotar

Mama Quilla

The ancient Incas revered the supreme moon goddess, Mama Quilla. As "Mother Moon," Mama Quilla is a protector of children and is associated with the passage of time and marriage. Her human features are set inside a silvery disk that shines brightly upon the Andean Mountains. Regular rituals and festivals were held in Mama Quilla's honor, and a lunar calendar was established in accordance with her changing appearance.

Women looked to Mama Quilla as a strong, benevolent advocate for their needs. The lunar deity assisted women during childbirth and often guided them in matters concerning fertility. She was worshipped in temples during the time of the Incan empire, the most famous structure being Coricancha of Cuzco. Mama Quilla was thought to be the mother of the first Inca king.

Mama Quilla's presence in the night skies was juxtaposed by her brother/husband Inti's daily appearance. Inti was the sun god who traveled across the sky and plunged into the western horizon. Upon his exit from the heavens, Mama Quilla would show her bright, silvery disk and rule the night skies.

Other deities surrounded the moon goddess and sun god with rainbows, thunder, lightning, planets, and stars. The planets and stars tended to Mama Quilla's needs as she engaged in the busy task of being moon goddess and protector of women.

During lunar eclipses, Mama Quilla's worshippers were particularly devoted to honoring their "Mother Moon." They feared she could fall into a rage or be devoured by a jaguar as a result of her temporary disappearance. It was also thought that a solar eclipse reflected Inti's bad temper and often portended misfortune.

Guided Meditation

Imagine you are lost in a lush rain forest. A cacophony of animal sounds assaults your senses. Gigantic wet leaves slap your face as you stumble through the darkness. You stop in your tracks and close your eyes, feeling paralyzed with fear. When you open your eyes, there stands before you the luminescence of Mama Quilla. She takes your hand and leads you to a trail illuminated by her lunar light. You see a beautiful display of orchids, bromeliads, and other jewels of the forest hanging from the vine-covered trees. A soft drumming commences and the animals chime in with their night sounds. Soon, your heart beats in sync with the hum of the forest, and you begin to feel as if you are part of the surroundings. You join the animal pageantry in the celebration of the goddess who is the mother of all the creatures. You feel safe with her light showing you the way through the wilderness. A jaguar comes up to you and strokes your leg with its soft coat. You feel its wild energy as it joins you on your journey. The forest is alive with celebration in the presence of the feminine divine. Look up and see the beautiful array of stars. Suddenly a comet shoots across the sky. Close your eyes again and think of yourself as that comet. As you absorb the comet's bright energy, slowly bring yourself back to consciousness.

The goddess can help light your path
when you feel you have lost your way.
Do not fear the unknown; take charge
and be a trailblazer. Her light and
motherly love will help you to
see through the darkness.

Mama Quilla

Mawu

The Fon people of West Africa worshipped a supreme moon goddess who had created a landscape of mountains, valleys, and rivers by riding on the back of a sacred serpent. She formed people and animals from mud, and lit a great fire from the sky to bring light to the world and view her primordial creations. Upon viewing her work, she began to worry about taxing the Earth's fragile foundation with the growing burden of new life; therefore, she instructed the serpent deity Aido Hwedo to slither under the Earth's surface and hold it up so that it would never collapse under the weight.

Satisfied with the results of her labors, Mawu embraced the heavens, where she ruled the evening skies as a lunar deity. She shared the heavens with her twin, Lisa, the sun god. As children of the goddess Nanu Buluku, each twin had a different but important role to play in the cosmic order. As the moon goddess, Mawu guided people to rest and relaxation and refreshed the world with nocturnal coolness. Her sun god twin Lisa brought warmth and light during the daylight hours, allowing plants and life to thrive, but also exhausting mortals with his excessive heat. Together they maintained the balance of growth and rest, life and death. It is said that during an eclipse, the twins united and created seven sets of twins. The newly born deities contributed to the various elements of the universe.

Even though Mawu is regarded as a wise mother goddess who set life into motion, she is also associated with death. Mawu commanded respect from her mortals and she demanded that they honor *sekpoli*, which is the essence of one's life and is the soul force that connects all to the supreme goddess herself. When an insolent mortal named Awe challenged Mawu's power by attempting to create life from mud, he failed to provide the lifeless form with sekpoli. Conceding defeat, Awe accepted a bowl of cereal from Mawu, unaware that she had poisoned the porridge with the seed of death. As he digested the lethal seed, he understood the consequences of his arrogant behavior. This provided a reminder to humanity that the omnipotent goddess possessed not only the power to bring forth life but also to just as easily take it away.

Guided Meditation

Imagine yourself in a verdant valley with a backdrop of mountains. You are walking along the bank of a river. The moon lights your way. You see your own breath break through the crisp night air. A glow ahead invites you to explore the source of its illumination. You come upon a clearing and there stands the moon goddess Mawu. She beckons you to join her circle, where other goddesses have gathered to share the warmth of a fire. You see a snake, but it is a benevolent snake creating beautiful spirals in the sand. You contemplate the spirals while you join hands with the goddesses and circle 'round the fire. The glow of the fire moves through your body. You feel the circle of deities levitating around you. You are part of this floating circle and soon you feel your body enveloped by stars. You can no longer define the separation between earth and sky. Fire and star energy become one. Bask in this energy and experience the infinite nature of life. As your body begins to descend back to Earth, feel yourself return to consciousness.

The goddess can show you that the
continuous nature of life facilitates changes.
Embrace every stage with the knowledge
that there are no endings, just new
situations and opportunities.

Tawu

Nut

The Egyptian goddess of the sky, Nut is personified as the heavens and is incubator of the clouds and stars. She has many manifestations and is associated with the cow, sow, sycamore tree, and the Milky Way. She is the daughter of Shu and Tefnut, and sister to the Earth god Seb.

Nut is a complex deity who rose from primordial waters, became the lover of Seb, and eventually metamorphosed into the sky. Ra, the sun god who represented light, was enraged by Nut's incestuous affair with Seb and ordered Shu, who represented air, to separate the two by forming a bridge between them. As a result, Nut could only look upon her lover, who formed the mountains and valleys on the planes below. Nut is often depicted as an arched form whose arms and legs acted as supporting pillars. The pillars represented the four cardinal points and symbolized wholeness. She was sometimes shown shedding heavenly tears that rained down upon the Earth.

It is said that the sun makes its daily journey by entering the mouth of Nut and then traveling through her body until he is reborn from her womb. The daily delivery of sunrise and sunset symbolizes the cycle of life. Nut is the great mistress of heaven, whose body is the essence of renewal and continuation. She is also the protector of the dead and is often depicted spreading her wings on the lids of Egyptian coffins. Hieroglyphics pertaining to the goddess were inscribed on the sarcophagi of the deceased as a means of appealing to the great sky goddess. Her position as the heavenly deity offered comfort and support for the dead, who were in need of guidance and care.

Nut gave birth to five deities born on either a lucky or unlucky day within the five epagonmenal days of the extended Egyptian year. Nut's most important and well-known child is Isis, who arrived on a "lucky day" and was the subject of a long-lasting cult that made her one of the most beloved goddesses of all time.

Guided Meditation

You are levitating toward the heavens. Before you is a carpet of brilliant stars. As you approach the stars, you see that they comprise the form of Nut. Her body arches over you with its luminosity. You feel a warmth travel through your fingertips as you reach out to touch her. The heat travels from your hand, to your arm, and throughout your body until, finally, you feel warmth flood your subconscious. The subconscious is an open universe containing goddess energy. Allow yourself to slip into this universe. Each star contains goddess energy and information necessary for self-empowerment. Allow all negative thoughts to slip out of your body as you melt into a sea of stars. Touch the stars and gather stardust while contemplating the goddess. The divine dust will help you along your journey in the subconscious. You are ready to reenter the conscious area of your mind carrying the gathered dust of knowledge. You break through layers of clouds and descend down to Earth. Feel your body materialize. When your body touches the warm ground, feel yourself return to consciousness.

By accessing your internal divine contained
in the subconscious, you can learn to
travel the sea of stars where much
collective information is stored.
We can become more aware of both
ourself and those around us if we
learn to harness this energy
in a positive manner.

Nut

Pana

The Palermuit and Caribou Inuit peoples revere a spirit in the sky known as Pana, or "Woman Up There." Pana acts as temporary custodian for souls who traverse from the middle world known as Earth to her upper realms in the star-laden sky. Under her care, souls are reincarnated and are then returned to the middle world to be reborn again in babies.

The Inuit believe that there are several layers of existence. There is the underworld where evil spirits dwell, the middle world where mortals coexist with the harsh elements on the Earth's upper crust, and then there is the upper-world where souls travel to after exiting their mortal shells. During the soul's sojourn, Pana, with the help of the moon, readies the new arrivals for their journey back to mortal soil. While the moon assists Pana's efforts to return souls to Earth, he is unable to shine, thus explaining the absence of the illuminated orb at certain times. Pana's home in the sky is full of holes. Sometimes particles from the upper world slip through these openings and rain down upon the Earth in the form of snow or hail. It is also thought that the aurora borealis had poured through the celestial plane to paint the sky with its beautiful, bright hues.

The Inuit often attempted to converse with the spirits that inhabit the upper and lower worlds by consulting a shaman. A shaman was able to assume a trancelike state that enabled him to traverse between the various planes of existence and engage in dialog with powerful, ethereal beings. Communicating with the spirits helped mortals cope with illness and other life-threatening situations. Pana's connection with immortality and weather made her an important host for the shaman's visitations. Maintaining good standing with Pana assured the continuation of life and cosmic balance.

Guided Meditation

Imagine glistening icicle clusters. They form mirrors reflecting an infinite number of refracted faces. You travel through an icy cavern in the company of images from your past. Each icicle has its own unique shape, yet it is part of the whole ice formation that comprises your surroundings. Waves of color catch your attention and you see an opening at the end of an ice tunnel. You walk into the tunnel and experience a vortex of snow spinning into a kaleidoscope of glorious colors. You feel the pull of the vortex drawing your body out of the tunnel. You are flying free amidst the dazzling display of color and light. Absorb the cosmic energy from the dancing aurora borealis and concentrate on how you can manifest this energy into your conscious being. Observe the showcase before you and feel that your dreams are achievable in the cosmic order of light and energy. Pana appears amidst these images and nods to you. She approves of your dreams and is willing to embrace them with you. Go to her and let yourself be held in her reassuring arms. She kisses your forehead and you are now ready to return to your conscious state.

Dreams are as continuous as life itself.
The goddess supports your dreams and
helps you to realize that your visions are
unique in the cosmic dance of life.

Pana

Saule

The Slavic sun goddess of the heavens is worshipped for her life-giving warmth and light. Saule presides over the heavens in her cloud-filled domain and pours golden light from a jug down to the people of Earth. A compassionate deity, Saule cares for orphans and other forgotten souls. She is a nurturing mother who aids in all kinds of activities, including weaving, spinning, and music. She is adorned in clothing embroidered in silvers and golds as she rides the sky in her chariot. Her celestial powers fill the landscape with greenery and beauty. In the colder regions of Europe, Saule's cascading golden rays are a welcome relief to the harsh winters that often paralyze the land. Her blessing brings hope and light and ensures the continuation of the life cycle.

Saule is associated with a green snake that she wears on her crown as a symbol of fertility. It was widely believed that treating a green snake with kindness was a means of ensuring fecundity and wealth. But if one were to injure or kill the benevolent reptile, bad luck would prevail. Some even believed that to cast eyes upon a dead green snake was to initiate sadness in the sun goddess and possibly bring about coldness and darkness upon the world. Many worshippers of the sun goddess kept a green snake in the household as a means of good luck and protection. Their reverence for the snake was a means of honoring and respecting the sun goddess herself.

The moon god Meness was the sun goddess' consort. Together they bore Earth, their beautiful daughter. After separating, the moon god and the sun goddess divided the responsibility of keeping a watchful eye on Earth.

Guided Meditation

You are standing in a pasture dotted with budding wildflowers. Birds are singing softly amidst a magnificent landscape of snow-capped mountains, pine trees, and rolling pastures. You raise your arms as though you are about to embrace a fluffy cloud. Close your eyes, breathe deeply, and feel the rays of sun caress you like a warm liquid that pours over your body. Your mind feels cleansed and your body is reenergized. You open your eyes and see Saule standing before you. She hands you a jug filled with the golden liquid of the sun. You take a drink and feel yourself merging with the solar energy. Any residual cold, dark, negative feelings drain from your body, allowing the new energy to take its place. The freshness of springtime thaws your cold bones and enables you to see clearly. You can see the details on the distant mountain. You can see the snow melting off the rocky precipices. You watch a bird building its nest in a nearby tree. The blooms of flowers are opening more fully and you feel compelled to pick one and smell its fresh fragrance. Everything around you is alive and you are part of the new season of change. Break into a dance, make a crown of flowers, and allow your senses to reawaken. Hold out your arms to the burgeoning world around you and slowly bring yourself back to consciousness.

Sometimes an incubation period is necessary
before we can fully embrace
new ideas and directions.

Saule

Selene

The lovely Greek moon goddess Selene rides across the evening sky aboard a silver chariot led by two magnificent white steeds. From this perch, Selene leaves streams of light along her path, thus illuminating Earth with her presence. Her hair and robe whip in the wind as she eagerly rides the celestial currents. Selene is sometimes depicted with wings and a golden diadem with a crescent moon. She takes her position as the orb in the night sky after her brother Helios, the sun god, completes his daily journey. Selene is the daughter of the Titan Hyperion and the goddess Theia, and thus she inherited a divine position in the skies.

Selene fell in love with a handsome mortal shepherd named Endymion and seduced him while he was sleeping in his cave. From then on, Selene made nightly sojourns to Asia Minor, where her lover resided. Over many years their passionate love affair resulted in the birth of fifty daughters.

Endymion's mortal shell was subject to aging, thus Selene granted Endymion's wish for eternal beauty. As a price for everlasting youth, Endymion had to remain asleep even during romantic interludes under Selene's lunar light. Every night, Selene visits her dreaming lover and brushes his face with affectionate kisses.

Selene is associated with elements of the evening sky, including the moon, stars, and planets. She is regarded as a goddess who brings romance to the hearts of sleeping mortals. Her sensual beauty lures many to her loving embrace, and thus she has become the subject of much love poetry.

Guided Meditation

You are floating listlessly in space. It is dark, cold, and lonely in your marooned state. You are paralyzed and unsure how to remove yourself from peril. You spot a light in the far distance but it is difficult for you to make out what it is. Your eyes are unused to bright light and it takes you a moment to focus. It is the goddess Selene on her chariot. You wave to her and she guides her chariot to your side. She smiles and beckons you to climb aboard. You look upon the goddess and she smiles gently. You feel a pulse of energy travel through you and soon your fear lessens, allowing you to climb aboard the chariot. Selene whips the reins and the chariot resumes flight. The goddess commands her vehicle with strength and determination. Her willfulness and self-assurance make you feel more confident and relaxed. The white steeds break through the darkness and gallop onto new cosmic planes. Planetary bodies, stars, and comets are spread out endlessly before you. You become so mesmerized by the sights and sounds that you have forgotten your fears. You can feel your limbs loosen up and your mind break free of the chains that had imprisoned you before embarking on this journey with Selene. Feel the strength of the stars fortify your being. With the goddess, there is nothing you cannot do and nowhere you cannot go. Breathe deeply and feel your body return to consciousness.

The goddess can help you break
the chains of fear that keep you
from pursuing your dreams.

Selene

Tara

One of the most popular and complex deities in the Buddhist tradition is Tara. Her name can translate to "Star" or "She Who Brings Us to the Other Shore." Tara is the goddess who navigates through the waters between darkness and light. She helps mortals obtain enlightenment and her strong, compassionate presence is often called upon during times of distress and endangerment. She is a savior goddess who assumes many forms and incarnations that shift and overlap and are assimilated into different cultures.

Tara is one of the oldest deities of Asia, and her influence is evident in the myriad of stories that have surfaced throughout the world. Her most recognized forms are "White Tara" or Sitatora and "Green Tara" or Symmatara. In Tibet, she is the bodhisattva and wife of Avalokitesvara. As the wife of a Buddha, some say she was born from a compassionate tear shed by Avalokitesvara just before he reached Nirvana. She then transformed into a powerful, compassionate energy who won the hearts and boundless devotion of her followers.

In Hinduism, Tara is a celestial goddess who was abducted by Soma, the moon. Tara's husband Brihaspati, the planet Jupiter, outraged by the kidnapping, called on Brahma to orchestrate her release. After attempts at reasoning with Soma failed, a war between the gods broke out. Eventually Soma capitulated to Brahma's demands and released a now-pregnant Tara. Eventually Tara gave birth to a beautiful, powerful child that caused both Brihaspati and Soma to claim fatherhood. It was revealed that the newborn, named Buddha, was the child of the moon, and he thus became the planet Mercury.

Tara is connected with light and is often depicted as a gentle, playful goddess.

Guided Meditation

Sit in the lotus position and relax. You begin to float in a sky where beams of light lift your body through layers of clouds. Feel the clouds caress your skin with mist. The movement ceases and your body now rests gently upon a cloud that feels soft as a pillow. A bright light blinds you for a moment before you are able to open your eyes to see Tara sitting opposite you. She is emanating pure energy and light and you feel your body absorbing the warmth from this powerful goddess. Her jewels are pieces of stars that cascade down her chest in a netting of sparkles. Breathe in and allow the bright energy to fill your veins with purity. The netting of stars expands and reaches out to you. Allow the stars to cloak your body with their healing properties. As you exhale, all negativity exits your body. Each star that is touching your body is helping you to feel relaxed, renewed, and rejuvenated. Soak in this good energy and continue to breathe. When you feel completely cleansed, your body will start to lower itself. Feel yourself descend through clouds and sky before returning to consciousness.

Harness your inner light with the help
of the goddess. You are connected to the stars
and have the capacity to draw energy from
them during times of need. It is important
to allow the new energy to replace negative
energy in order to maintain balance
in your internal cosmos.

Tara

Unelanuhi

The Cherokee worship the sun goddess Unelanuhi by bowing to her as she rises in the sky and casts golden light upon the plains. Her name means "Apportioner of Time" because it is her routine passage across the sky that marks the seasons and allows observers to bear witness to the passing of each day. Her position in the sky indicates what season is approaching and therefore the native peoples can make the appropriate preparations for climatic change. Unelanuhi epitomizes radiant beauty, strength, and power.

Unelanuhi was not always casting light upon the Earth's surface. It took the ingenious actions of Grandmother Spider to help place the sun in the sky. By weaving her web, Grandmother Spider was able to haul Unelanuhi into the heavens, thus allowing Earth to thrive under the golden rays of the sun goddess.

Unelanuhi keeps a watchful eye over the people who worship her from below. She is a healing goddess who aids those who need assistance. But she can also induce headaches and fever and is sometimes entreated during medicinal rituals to help restore health for the sick.

A mysterious visitor took Unelanuhi to be his lover and once a month they would have a rendezvous. Because his countenance was obscured by darkness, Unelanuhi rubbed ash on the stranger's face in hopes of discovering his true identity in the morning. When light revealed that it was her brother, the moon, whose concupiscence had wooed her, he fled in shame and waned into a thin crescent. But as he grows more conspicuous with the passing month, one can see the telltale signs of his illicit affair by the ash stains that still mark the moon's surface.

Guided Meditation

Watch the sun rise and gaze upon an enormous web that begins to form in the sky. The web extends down to the Earth. Impulsively you decide to climb the silken ropes. You climb toward the sun and allow the warm breezes to whip your hair and warm your body. You begin to feel tired on your journey and decide to look down. The web is infinite above and below your body. You feel disoriented and you begin to panic. The sun goddess comes to your aid and holds her arms out to you. You reach out to her and before you can fall, she takes your hand. She tells you to rid yourself of lingering problems. You imagine the weighty, troubling thoughts flooding out of your mind and dissipating into the cosmic void. Feel yourself lighten and soon you are able to take a firm hold of the web again. Pause on your journey and fortify yourself with thoughts of a new day, a new beginning, and the connective nature of the intricate web that you are climbing. Allow your body to slowly return to consciousness.

Life is a series of interconnected threads.
We all share this thread. You can affect
the universal web by your actions.
Trust in the goddess to help you purge
any heaviness that can damage the web
and hinder your climb.

Unelanuhi

Ushas

As a Hindu goddess of dawn, Ushas heralds the new day with light from her shining breasts that she reveals by parting her veils. She is an all-seeing goddess associated with wealth, cosmic order, and immortality. She is the light that drives away dark and thus is an important participant in the cosmic balance and passage of time. Many honor her as a propitious deity whose worship is said to promote strength and longevity.

Ushas' luminous beauty and grace has been celebrated by the Vedic poets through generations of oral tellings. She was written about in one of the oldest Hindu texts, the *Rig-Veda*. In this ancient Sanskrit work, deities and their powers are honored in beautifully composed poems and hymns.

Adorning herself in splendid red veils and gold jewelry, she rides on an illuminated chariot led by red cows or horses. Her magnificence emblazons the dark sky, awakening mortals below and assisting birds into morning flight. It is her welcoming presence that sets each subsequent day into flowing motion and keeps darkness from oppressing all those that feed on the energy emitted by her brilliance.

Ushas shares the sky with her sisters, two stars that appear before Ushas' arrival. She is also consort and mother to the sun god, Surya. Ushas and her family all play an important role in the maintenance of the diurnal cycle and the continuance of life. But it is Ushas herself who carries the daily torch of renewal with her faithful appearance in the eastern horizon. She is the immortal maiden of time who never ages, and yet her daily travels across the morning sky are a reminder to mortals that they continue to grow older with each passing day.

Guided Meditation

Imagine yourself adorned in layers of translucent silk veils. You are standing on the beach, watching the white waves rolling over sand. You begin to dance and twirl, with your veils flowing in the ocean breeze. A beautiful sunrise basks your dancing form with golden light. The sound of the ocean fills you with peace and equilibrium. You see Ushas emerge from the waves wearing her golden robes. Her light warms the air and sand. She joins your dance and you fall into perfect synchronicity. You feel the power of the goddess leading your feet in a cadence to the ocean waves, and soon you merge with the goddess. You feel the pulse of the universe reawaken your senses. The power of the waves fills your being with a sense of confidence and self-empowerment. There is nothing you cannot accomplish. The presence of the new morning sun rekindles your inner passions. Feel the dance begin to slow. Face the ocean with open arms and take a deep breath of the salty sea air. Exhale and slowly return to your conscious being.

Ushas is a reminder that each day represents
a new opportunity to acquaint yourself
with inner passions. It is never too late
to act on your desires.

Ushas

White Shell Woman

White Shell Woman, also known as "Yolkai Estsan," is a Navaho moon goddess. She was born amidst rainbow colors from an abalone shell. As a primordial creator goddess, White Shell Woman was responsible for creating woman and man from yellow and white ears of corn. She blessed these new beings with maize and fecundity and helped the mortals sustain life with nourishing rain. With each new dawn she welcomed the beings with her presence in the east. The goddess ruled over the white dawn and the ocean, and was an important force in maintaining the cycle of life.

Her sisters also presided over the seasonal cycles under the guidance of the all-powerful Changing Woman. Some say that White Shell Woman was a younger aspect of Changing Woman, and that her association with dawn represents new life. As the sun travels across the sky, she metamorphoses to become the crone Changing Woman at the end of the diurnal cycle. Others say White Shell Woman was Changing Woman herself in one of her many guises, and that she changed costume to accommodate the time of day.

There was an old Navaho tale of the days before humans knew fire. White Shell Woman sought to bring light to the world by encircling herself with turquoise and shells. She stood in the middle of her self-made ring and held a crystal. She concentrated on the crystal and allowed its powers to ignite a radiant flame that she then gave to the people below. The power of fire helped the people see through the darkness that covered their world after the sun sank below the horizon.

Guided Meditation

You are standing in a field of ripe corn. The aroma fills your senses and the white silk is tangled in your hair. You have lost your way in the endless rows. A shining light acts as a beacon beyond the field. You run toward it, brushing past the corn husks along the way. When you finally reach the end of the field, there stands White Shell Woman in the center of a circle. The circle is aglow with crystals. She gestures you to join the circle. You lift your foot over the crystals and feel a surge of energy travel up your spine. You allow your whole body to step forward as an energy force field envelops your body. The goddess holds a glowing crystal out to you. You place your hands over hers and feel the nourishment fill your veins with star energy. You sit down with her in the circle and together you pop corn. Gaze upon the kernels and see stars within the golden nuggets. You eat the popped corn until you feel full, content, and at peace with your being. Close your eyes and slowly bring yourself back to consciousness.

The goddess can provide you with the proper nourishment needed to confront new ideas, new possibilities, and to help combat old fears. Allow her to help you tend to your internal fields in the subconscious where a wealth of ideas, knowledge, and wisdom is waiting to be harvested.

White Shell Woman

Wuriupranili

The Aborigine people, who have inhabited Australia for over forty thousand years, revere the very soil where ancestral spirits awoke from their earthly wombs and helped to shape the world. These deities wandered through what is known as the Dreamtime, leaving evidence of their sacred path in the form of rocks, trees, and waterholes. The Aborigines continue to honor the myths that help to explain the origins of their surroundings, and they look to the sky to embrace the power of the sun goddess who continues to warm the sacred red earth with her daily visits.

The sun goddess Wuriupranili is part of this eternal Dreamtime. Every morning her flaming bark is a beacon for the new day as she slowly emerges from the eastern horizon and travels across the sky. As Wuriupranili rises into the heavens, she dusts her body with red ochre, allowing the clouds to capture the powdery residue and reflect the hue of the goddess' skin.

Upon reaching her westerly destination, she again applies the red ochre on her body to color a sunset landscape. The warm colors that embody the sky and earth mirror the dazzling goddess herself. Wuriupranili departs from view by submerging her torch into the waters below. The still-glowing embers of the bark help Wuriupranili to descend underground, allowing her to return east during the night under the protection of the Earth.

Wuriupranili's role as the sun goddess is a vital part of the continuation of life and the cosmos. Her appearance is a reminder to the Aborigine people that Dreamtime is not bound by a timeline but is an inherent part of the universe.

Guided Meditation

Imagine yourself standing on a vast plain of brush and red rock. You feel a dusting of red ochre covering your limbs with a rich, earthy scent. Wuriupranili appears with her torch and takes you on her cosmic tour. You climb the sky together, feeling the ochre leaving warm, colored streaks behind your ascending forms. You and the goddess are painting the sky with brilliant hues. You climb higher and fly over the vast ocean. You see whales jumping through the air and landing with majestic power and grace onto the waves. Dolphins leap and frolic in a synchronized display of water acrobatics. You see the color of the sky reflecting in the water and ponder the connective nature of water and sky. You feel yourself mimicking the exuberant dance of the sea creatures as you continue to accompany the goddess across the sky. You begin to descend toward the water. The red ochre of your bodies reflects into the water and you can identify your image in the ripples. The goddess holds out her torch to you and together you slowly immerse it into the water. The power from the extinguishing flame travels through your reflection. The ochre dusting melts into the water, enabling you to merge with the reflection. As warm water covers your body, listen to the soothing sound of the lapping waves. Breathe deeply and slowly bring yourself back to consciousness.

Your internal flame can never be extinguished.
Let the power that resides within aid you
toward self-realization. When you acquire
a better sense of self, you will be able to
light the way for others more readily.

Wuriupranili

Selected Bibliography

Arden, Harvey. *Dreamkeepers*. New York, N.Y.: Harper Collins Publishers, 1994.

Ardinger, Barbara. *Goddess Meditations*. St. Paul, Minn.: Llewellyn Publications, 1998.

Aveni, Anthony. *Stairways to the Stars*. New York, N.Y.: John Wiley & Sons, Inc., 1997.

Babcock, Michael, and Susan Seddon Boulet. *The Goddess Paintings*. Rohnert Park, Calif.: Pomegranate Artbooks, 1994.

Bell, Robert E. *Women of Classical Mythology*. New York, N.Y.: Oxford University Press, 1991.

Berresford, Peter Ellis. *Dictionary of Celtic Mythology*. New York, N.Y.: Oxford University Press, 1992.

Bierlein, J. F. *Parallel Myths*. New York, N.Y.: Ballantine Books, 1994.

Bonheim, Jajala (ed.). *Goddess: A Celebration in Art & Literature*. New York, N.Y.: Stewart, Tabori & Chang, 1997.

Brueton, Diana. *Many Moons*. New York, N.Y.: Prentice Hall, 1991.

Budge, E. A. Wallis. *The Gods of the Egyptians*. New York, N.Y.: Dover Publications, 1969.

Campbell, Joseph. *The Hero with a Thousand Faces*. Princeton, N.J.: Princeton University Press, 1949.

Conway, D. J. *Maiden, Mother, Crone*. St. Paul, Minn.: Llewellyn Publications, 1994.

Cotterwell, Arthur. *Celtic Mythology*. New York, N.Y.: Lorenz Books, 1999.

———. *A Dictionary of World Mythology*. New York, N.Y.: Oxford University Press, 1979.

———. *The Macmillan Illustrated Encyclopedia of Myths & Legends*. New York, N.Y.: Macmillan Publishing Co., 1989.

———. *Norse Mythology*. New York, N.Y.: Lorenz Books, 1999.

Cunningham, Scott. *Hawaiian Religion & Magic*. St. Paul, Minn.: Llewellyn Publications, 1994.

Danielou, Alain. *The Myths of Gods of India*. Rochester, N.Y.: Inner Traditions, 1985.

Gibson, Clare. *Goddess Symbols*. New York, N.Y.: Barnes & Noble, 1998.

Gill, D. Sam, and Irene F. Sullivan. *Dictionary of Native American Mythology*. New York, N.Y.: Oxford University Press, 1992.

Grimal, Pierre (ed.). *Larousse World Mythology*. New York, N.Y.: Hamlyn Publishing Group, 1968.

Gleiser, Marcelo. *The Dancing Universe: From Creation Myths to the Big Bang*. New York, N.Y.: Dutton Books, 1997.

Hallam, Elizabeth (ed.). *Gods and Goddesses: A Treasury of Deities and Tales from World Mythology*. New York, N.Y.: Macmillan, 1996.

Hamilton, Edith. *Mythology*. Boston, Mass.: Little Brown & Co., 1998.

Hunt, Norman Bancroft. *Gods and Myths of the Aztecs: The History and Development of Mexican Culture*. New York, N.Y.: Smithmark Publishers, 1996.

Husain, Shahrukh. *The Goddess*. London: Duncan Baird Publishers, 1997.

Imel, Martha Ann, et al. *Goddesses in World Mythology*. New York, N.Y.: Oxford University Press, 1993.

Jordan, Michael. *Encyclopedia of Gods*. New York, N.Y.: Facts on File, 1993.

Jung, Carl G. *The Archetypes of the Collective Unconscious*. Princeton, N.J.: Princeton University Press, 1990.

Kennedy, Mike Dixon. *Native American Myth and Legend: An A–Z of People and Places*. London: A Blandford Book, 1996.

Kinsley, David R. *Hindu Goddesses*. Berkeley and Los Angeles, Calif.: University of California Press, 1988.

Krupp, E. C. *Beyond the Blue Horizon: Myths and Legends of the Sun, Moon, Stars, and Planets*. New York, N.Y.: Oxford University Press, 1991.

Leeming, David, and Jake Page. *Goddess: Myths of the Feminine Divine*. New York, N.Y.: Oxford University Press, 1994.

Levi-Strauss, Claude. *Myth and Meaning*. New York, N.Y.: Shocken Books, 1979.

MacCana, Proinsias. *Celtic Mythology*. New York, N.Y.: Peter Bedrick Books, 1983.

Mercantante, Anthony S. *World Mythology and Legend*. New York, N.Y.: Facts on File, 1988.

Miller, Sherrill, and Courtney Milne. *Visions of the Goddess*. New York, N.Y.: Penguin Studios, 1998.

Monaghan, Patricia. *The New Book of Goddesses & Heroines*. St. Paul, Minn.: Llewellyn Publications, 1998.

Neumann, Erich. *The Great Mother*. Princeton, N.J.: Princeton University Press, 1991.

O'Neill, Cynthia (ed.). *Goddesses, Heroes and Shamans*. New York, N.Y.: Larousse Kingfisher Chambers Inc., 1994.

Parrinder, Geofrey. *African Mythology*. New York, N.Y.: Peter Bedrick Books, 1982.

Phillip, Neil. *The Illustrated Book of Myths*. New York, N.Y.: Dorling Kindersley Publishing, 1995.

Stone, Merlin. *Ancient Mirrors of Womanhood*. Boston, Mass.: Beacon Press, 1990.

Walker, Barbara G. *The Women's Encyclopedia of Myths and Secrets*. Edison, N.J.: Castle Books, 1996.

Wilson, Edward O. *Consilience: The Unity of Knowledge*. New York, N.Y.: Alfred A. Knopf, 1998.

Websites that were helpful:

www.nasa.gov

www.pantheon.org/mythica.html